The Way Things Were

By Margaret Clyne
and Rachel Griffiths

CELEBRATION PRESS
Pearson Learning Group

At Home

Years ago some kitchens looked like this.

Today some kitchens look like this.

At School

Years ago some classrooms looked like this.

Today some classrooms look
like this.

At Play

Years ago some playtimes looked like this.

Today some playtimes look
like this.

Years Ago   ## Today

Talk About It

1. How do the photographs help you understand the book?

2. Look at page 8. How are some things from years ago like things today? How are they different?

3. How are you different from the way you were as a baby? Explain.

Word count: 39

DRA® Level	4
Guided Reading Level	C
Intervention Level	4

Nonfiction Genre
Informational

Content Area
History

Comprehension Skill
Compare and Contrast

Nonfiction Features
Headings, Picture Chart

How did things look yesterday? How do they look today? *The Way Things Were* shows how life has stayed the same and how it is different.

1-800-321-3106
www.pearsonlearning.com

ISBN 0-7652-5148-5

Natkhat
the naughty
Monkey